PLAYS FOR ONE PERSON

David Pownall

PLAYS FOR ONE PERSON

ROUSSEAU'S TALE

CRATES ON BARRELS

LATER

OBERON BOOKS

LONDON

First published in 2003 by Oberon Books Ltd.
(incorporating Absolute Classics)
521 Caledonian Road, London N7 9RH
Tel: 020 7607 3637 / Fax: 020 7607 3629

e-mail: oberon.books@btinternet.com
www.oberonbooks.com

A catalogue record for this book is available from the British
Library.

ISBN: 1 84002 010 5

Cover design: Andrzej Klimowski

Printed in Great Britain by Antony Rowe Ltd, Chippenham.

Contents

ROUSSEAU'S TALE

Rousseau's Tale was first performed at The Cockpit, Marylebone, London on 11 October 1990 by Stephen Boxer, directed by Stephen Daldrey, as part of the Not The RSC Festival.

It is imagined that in 1765 Jean-Jaques Rousseau, exiled from him native France, has been invited by the Royal Society to deliver a lecture on the subject of his sexual feelings. Soon afterwards he will begin writing his *Confessions*.

1765.

The premises of the Royal Society, Crane Court, Fleet Street, London. A beautiful, ornate lit candelabra with a Louis Quatorze chair beside it.

Using a stick, dressed in a kaftan, jacket, baggy trousers, boots and belt, ROUSSEAU at fifty-three clumps onto the stage. He pauses, then throws his stick off, dropping a notebook and pencil, muttering to himself. His hair sticks out from under a wig which is awry. However, within his stumbling and peasantish affectations lurk the manners of a sophisticate – and a French sophisticate at that. When he bends over to pick up the notebook and pencil it is done with an absurdly formal grace.

Throwing off his hat and coat, he dumps them on the floor, then wipes his face with a handkerchief. This is done with care and a few flourishes. Suddenly he crumples the handkerchief into a ball and stuffs it into his pocket. He contacts the audience with his eyes for the first time. Shaking his head, he sits down and looks into his notebook, holding up a hand as if to say: 'Give me a moment to myself.' Getting to his feet, he speaks:

ROUSSEAU: My lords, gentlemen, fellows and members, I was charmed by your invitation to address this August company, and pleased by the pecuniary inducements to do so. The Royal Society has much more money than I have and hardly less reputation for intellectual talent. That you should pay Jean-Jacques Rousseau in order to meet him, as well as for his insights and philosophy is appropriate: that I, knowing more and having suffered more than any of you, should accept your generosity means that the balance between desserts and abilities can be redressed for as long as I am here, on my feet, giving

9

you my all. When it is over the inequalities and injustices that plague our world will resume their paramountcy. I hope we leave this place better citizens, having been coupled with Truth for a while. So, I salute your money, I cherish your hospitality, and I curse my own penury which has brought me before you, a performer! And in what an absurdly unfashionable costume this performer presents himself! How pretentious! If I tell you it's the national costume of the men of Armenia, that doesn't help, does it? I've never been near Armenia – nor am I likely to – but the formal attire people of quality in France and England are expected to wear is far too tight and restrictive for me – unhealthy – cutting off the blood, putting excessive pressure on the bladder. A man suffering pressure on his bladder should emigrate to Armenia and be comfortable – sadly, I doubt if they'd let an old political chatterbox like me over the border.

To study me closely must be a curious pleasure for you. You must be surprised and that is always an enjoyable sensation. So, this is Jean-Jacques Rousseau! What is all the fuss about? This ordinary person has caused all that trouble? There must be some reason why I am an outcast from the country that I love. The king of France has not forced me into exile for nothing. I am reckoned to be a seditious, dangerous man. That, I would deny. Peace is my primary concern. But I am an interesting man; informative, perhaps opinionated, serious, tender, sincere even amusing.

And, be certain, I will entertain you! But I will torment you no longer by pretending that I am ignorant of the hopes that you entertain of me. It is not my views on logic which you seek, nor my comments on the writing of essays or novels; nor my perceptions of political situations. What you want from me is my life of feelings. The President of the Royal Society was very clear.

Tonight will be a major event in the history of English civilisation! Tonight, in this room, before the thinkers and artists of England, a unique thing will be done by a unique man. The total truth will be told. Not of geometry, or astronomy, or any natural science, or history, but of the most poisoned, disguised and dishonest thing of all, and the most important – sexual feelings. That is what I am going to talk about. Not anyone's sexual feelings, but my own. Who else's can I explain? You have before you a man who still has his vigour: a virile man, a man of not unpleasing appearance; lithe, amiable, attractive to women would they were allowed to be here to confirm it!

Yes, I still have many attributes of youth, including the talent for arousing sexual desire in the opposite sex. It is important that I recognise these virtues in myself if my heroic attempt at self-knowledge in full public view is to be a success: for this is not only an entertainment for you but the first step in my experiments with self which will produce a full written confession of my life 'warts and all' as that great Englishman, Oliver Cromwell said to the man painting his portrait.

Before I embark on the detailed description of my sexual pilgrimage through life there is a warning that I must give you about myself. I am very vulnerable – an exile, a guest in this country, a poor man with little common sense; the quality that the English prize above all others. There is nothing common about me. All my senses are extraordinary. I compose music for kings. I write novels that shake governments. My philosophy is entirely my own. What is worrying to me is – have I any senses in common with other people at all? But I must believe that I have, otherwise I will doubt my own humanity, and that is the power which drives me through life.

To be a powerful influence upon the way other people think is a great responsibility. One can only comfort oneself by being convinced that, at least, you know that they must feel the same way but dare not express themselves. That is why sex is so important. If there is a common sense it is sex.

What I have done is to examine my sexual feelings and the activities that they have produced and then compared these to the general experience. I am not saying that my sexual feelings are right but only that they are there. It would surprise me if at the end of this evening there was a queue of people waiting to tell me that they have suffered to the same degree and in the same manner and have reached the same conclusions as myself. What I would like to know is whether my philosophy is justified in terms of any other person's feelings than my own. Are my feelings unique in the annals? Having listened to me one or two of you may think that you perceive a coincidence of feeling between us. If that is the case I will immediately want to know if those people have arrived at the same views about life. This is the vital connection. The vital question between us will then be – are our feelings natural? As you hear my account of my sexual development this is what I would like you to ponder on.

Environment is a vital part of any creation of emotion. I am talking to you in a language that is not your own, though you can speak it. I refuse to speak yours, though I can if I wish, because it is alien to me in spirit. My hatred of English as a barbaric, clumsy tongue which is of no use in philosophy or literature is part of the feeling with which I speak to you tonight. That will create a feeling in you and a final feeling will be produced between us.

If there is no justice in my Anglophobia – and I am here as a refugee from my own country, grateful for the protection and hospitality I have been afforded – can there be any justice in the feelings which I may incite in English people? My dislike of England is not a sexual feeling, though it is passionate, therefore we will not dwell on it; but it is a feeling nonetheless and it is only right that it should be taken into account.

I will not pause to explain why I loathe and detest England to such a degree: not even to mention such trivial things as your weather, your tedious and silly sense of humour, grasping empire, insensitive institutions, vicious laws. Oh, Voltaire may love you but I hate you! Is that because I hate Voltaire? Because I am French, your traditional enemy? All this is inappropriate now though it could be the subject of a second lecture should you decide to invite me back after this one.

Pause.

Well, at least you can start thinking about it. So, you are being addressed by a man who is unreliable in your terms – patriotism being a more popular virtue than goodness or honesty – and I must appear to be crippled by prejudice. If I suffer from such extravagant emotions about an idea – England is only an idea – does that not make it impossible for me to think clearly about a manifestation of my innermost self? Nothing breeds hatred like hatred. If I say I love you, you must warm to me. If I say that I hate you, you will be repelled.

Yet, though I hate you all as Englishmen and Englishwomen, I would feel differently about each one of you should we ever be locked in a room together and left to discover mutual feelings.

Ah, so that thought does excite you. Good. I admire enthusiasm. Now I hope you are intrigued because you find me a rough, simple, plain-speaking fellow with insufficient manners but an obvious intelligence. It must be clear to you now that I have integrity. No man bites that hand that feeds him unless he is very hungry. And I am very hungry for the truth.

Now, my sexual beginnings. As with all of us it was through that juvenile practice masturbation – a practice I still maintain in these, my nature years, and cannot break with. So, it not only has an allure for the childish experimenter testing the responses of his or her body, but also for someone who has tasted the full delights of sex with many partners of different qualities and skills, but who still persists in the lonely occupation of onanism. That is the kind of sorry creature who addresses you. You must be disgusted.

I need that. You are all intelligent people. My strategy is too obvious to disguise. I am trying to make sympathy impossible at this stage because sympathy makes me uncomfortable. Nor do I want to move too fast with you or make you like me. Be repelled a little. Victimise me. I make a good victim. It is a very privileged position from which to judge society. When I was a boy I was thrown onto the world as a sacrifice: my poor father was widowed and he could not maintain an interest in me, being more fascinated by clocks which function by laws less arbitrary than children. He gave me away as one might give away a broken toy: mend it, he said and it might come to some good. I was passed from hand to hand and many good, decent people used me as a servant or apprentice. Strangely enough it was the love of my life, Madame de Warens who was to use me worst. She sent me to Turin to be made into a Catholic. I had been born a good Geneva Protestant but the hospice for converts offered me money for my soul as the Devil did to Faustus and I accepted joining a class of villains, vagrants and desperados who had similarly signed away their hopes of redemption for nothing but lucre. Two of these ruffians were Croats who called themselves Jews or Moors and they had spent many years wandering through Spain and Italy being converted to Catholicism as often as possible. So, at a tender age, I was in company with the quintessence of deceit and ready to perjure my eternal soul.

If anything saved the integrity of my spirit during this dangerous time it was sex in its most abhorrent but cathartic form, sex that put religion into a dazzling perspective.

The sense of death and the sense of sex are awakened in us at the same time. To death comes religion as an anodyne: to sex, beauty which will refine and justify its savage source. At the point where I was about to commit an act of gross scepticism and betray the pure faith of my Protestant fathers, the soul of one of these filthy cut-throat Africans, whatever they were, came to my aid. The poor man took a fancy to me. At a crucial moment he demonstrated that his desire was not for God but for me and that was a cornerstone in the building of my philosophy.

The creature was unable to concentrate on his lessons. His habit was to find me wherever I was and try to converse in his tribal jargon. He did things for me to show his feelings and he kissed me often. These embraces displeased me but I put up with them out of friendship, even when they got out of control. All the time I was telling myself that this grown man is in the grip of some power more demanding than the divine. He cannot help himself. When the fellow wanted to share my bed so we could learn our religious lessons off the same pillow I demurred, giving as my reason the narrowness of my bed but not of my mind.

The next morning he contrived to find me alone in the assembly hall. He attacked me in the most direct manner, mad with lust. I broke away from him but without displaying indignation or anger. He then spent his seed upon the floor, helpless, so sad.

In my young life I had never seen this happen. I did not know what it was. All I knew was that this poor man could not hide it or lie about it as he could about his religious beliefs. There was a compulsion in this fury of Nature, a force that swept aside hypocrisy or greed. It frightened me so much that since then I have always been on my guard against pederasts and sympathised with women for having to face men in that state. I complained to the priests who refused to believe what I said. They did not want to lose the credit for converting an Arab, regardless of his disgusting sins. The crazed pederast was christened in white to symbolise the purity of his soul. I hated him then, this victim of unrestrained carnality, but now I have cause to thank him. He made it possible for me to seek a religion of my own that could absorb and comprehend his behaviour: also, he gave women greater value for me by way of contrast. I shouldered a debt that my gender owes them for the brutality of male concupiscence; a debt that can only be paid by the most delicate affection and personal homage.

It is my habit and discipline to be absolutely honest in these matters as with all concerns of human sensation and natural compulsions. It is a comfort to me to be able to speak with total frankness on this subject and have you completely aware of what I am talking about. However, there is a frisson in the air. A humming as of wings starting to beat – fly away, fly away. If there is anyone in the audience who can imagine him becoming affronted or ashamed by my directness and honesty then I suggested that they leave now rather than disturb the company at a point when I require its absolute, rapt attention. No one will think badly of you. The only comment that one might make is: ' – there goes someone with something to hide.'

Pause.

No? You have had your chance. Then, from now on I forbid anyone to leave under any pretext whatsoever as we are entering a sacred discourse between myself and my animal soul. Disgust and revulsion have no place here. We are in the temple of Truth.

Masturbation has several uses. Firstly, it is a course of natural instruction in the functioning of the pubescent body; secondly, it is a source of pleasure; and, thirdly, it has an industrial use as a manufactory of guilt. I must see my own history and addiction to it in the light of these three employments. But before I do that I must be more sharp and specific to the point that science requires. We must talk about instruments. In my case, as I am of the masculine gender, we must be particular.

When I discussed the aids and apparatus that I might need to illustrate my points, the President of the Royal Society kindly offered me a penis pickled in a jar. It had once belonged to a celebrated English criminal who was hanged and his body handed over to students of anatomy. But I refused the President's offer. Not because I had any contempt for the miscreant's member, but for the reason that it was not mine.

My sex is mine. A simple concept but one that is not generally appreciated. No man is more guilty of denying other people that crucial identity than I am. Others, I say, must fit my pattern. Their sex must have the quality of art that I appreciate. As our lives are hampered by laws and regulations unfitted for human happiness, so our minds respond. They come up with rules of their own which the most natural and unrestrainable essences cannot obey.

Twenty years ago I worked at the French embassy in Venice in a junior capacity. It is a city devoted to the pursuit of love, an emotion that it warps in practice and purifies through music in a regenerative cycle. Venice is like music: as insubstantial, as strange. It was there that I met the most beautiful woman whom I have ever encountered: Giulietta. It is in keeping with the character of Venice that this paragon should be a courtesan. No such woman could be a wife in that city.

She was charming, she was lively, a brunette, twenty at the most. She only spoke Italian and her accent alone would have been enough to turn my head. She had large, black, Oriental eyes that darted fiery sparks into my heart. Within an hour of meeting her I was her captive. I sat at a table with many other guests and listened to her as she boasted of the price that men put on her favours. 'When I go to bed with men whom I do not love, I make them pay for the boredom they cause me. What could be fairer than that?' she said.

This girl – for that is all she was – seemed to like me. I had no money. During the course of the evening I endeavoured to convey this to her. This enticing, sportive maid invited me to visit her anyway. I entered into a dream, of sensual delight and wished the hours away until my appointment.

Listen carefully. If you can follow the course of this episode and untangle the feelings that it discloses you will have advanced in your knowledge of Jean-Jacques Rousseau.

I entered her room as if it were a church. When I saw her it was the beauty of God that I looked upon. I could never have believed it possible that mere beauty could inspire me with such feelings of awe. As I approached her the driving passion that drove me suddenly declined and I felt a deathly cold flow through my veins. My legs trembled. I sat down on the point of fainting and wept like a child.

This woman was Nature's masterpiece. She was perfect, and she knew it. Not for a moment did she believe that repugnance for her profession or fear of the pox had anything to do with my weakness. She got up from her bed where she was lying half-clad, walked around the room, looked at herself in the mirror a few times, adjusted her hair, then came and sat next to me, uncovering her bosom so that I could put my troubled head upon it.

They were the breasts of a virgin. I felt as if I must be the first man to see them though my rational sense should have told that many hundreds had been cradled there. I experienced a thrill of relief and gratitude that this lovely, exquisite woman should be so compassionate when I had given her the opportunity to be insulted by my ineptitude. Never have I been closer to my dream of loving ecstasy than that moment when I bent to kiss her breast.

Then I saw that she had a deformed nipple. I halted my head and looked again, comparing it to the other one. They did not match. Groaning, I beat my brow with the palms of my hands and the tears started again. I found myself wondering how this remarkable imperfection had come about. This creature was a reject of Nature, a monster. I said to her, 'Giulietta, you have a deformed nipple. How did that happen?' This did not please her but she tried to make a joke about it, hoping that I would not mention it again. But I persisted, pointing out again and again that she was flawed.

Eventually she moved away and said coldly, 'Take my advice: give up the ladies and study mathematics.'

Sex is an urge shared by all living things in varying degrees of consciousness. I am acutely conscious of it because I am a human being. If I were a cockle-shell it would be a different experience: not necessarily any the less intense but certainly there would be no opportunity to apply intelligence. It is the application of that intelligence to sex that creates beauty. Beauty moves society, but so does oppression. I oppressed that kind-hearted Venetian prostitute because I had made her into something that she was not. She grew cold towards me as we must grow cold to those who wish to make this life beautiful at our expense.

So much beauty is kept alive by evasion. It cannot incorporate the ugly as complete love must do. There is the paradoxical penis to contend with. It is the least aesthetically pleasing part of a man's body. It disappoints the artist in us to the point where the Ancients could not bring themselves to give it a name of its own, they were so appalled at its lack of style. They called it a tail. Penis means tail. There must have been many surprises for Roman girls who trusted words. We need look no further for evidence of deceit and ambiguousness about sex.

If the Romans could not be direct about it then we must ask whether God did not intend Man to be in two minds about reproduction. Perhaps it is too close to God's exclusive power to create life and therefore a sin of pride.

Sexual feelings in the young child are pure. They are Nature's proof of the future. It is the time when sensations of unpolluted joy and excitement are created by puerile impotence, anticipating the power to copulate and inseminate. Religion has its source here: all refined ecstasy: all spiritual beauty. Masturbation, for me, was merely the endeavour of pushing forward the limits of my spiritual progress on my own, without the interference of teachers or guardians. After many years of youthful experiment I reached the point where I received the gift of physical ecstasy which had been the goal of all my efforts. But it was the spiritual pleasures that came first and informed the moment of my first ejaculation. With many boys this happens in sleep, induced by dreams, but with me it was brought about by hard work in full consciousness.

However, I cannot completely escape from the society which surrounds me. Although masturbation is the right of any person, free or enslaved, society still insists upon making a moral comment on it. We are not sent to a real prison to be punished: we are sent to a worse place – the penitentiary of guilt. This is a sentence that I have refused to accept.

As a man who acknowledges his status as a leading influence on the thought of powerful nations I have to confess that this small act of self-liberation is essential to my sanity. It is a statement of my need to be private, and my need to be free. That society should demand that I feel shame for this is more a comment on its moral values than on mine.

Although I have been in love many times I have not had much joy out of intercourse with women. The true pleasure of love with the female has proved to be more in the nature of a fusion of souls rather than bodies. I have tried to enjoy love at the highest levels both counts but the spiritual always outstrips the physical. With the women whom I have adored most intensely the act of love has always been a penance and I could have done without it if they could. This has created circumstances that condemned my affairs to tragic ends and separation. I do not include my marriage. That has lasted well. But my wife is low-born, not ambitious – she has not the talent or intellect to justify it – and she is a simple, strong, stupid woman of the best sort. I do not expect too much of her. She cannot share my highest thoughts. In twenty-five years she has not changed. She has all the loyalty and fondness that one might expect of an unsophisticated and uneducated woman of robust natural feelings who cannot interpret them or talk about them. I will never desert her for one of my more articulate and sensitive mistresses. She has had that assurance from me many times.

Our love has been natural though primitive and it is right that it has been the union in my life that has produced offspring. These children have been placed in foundling homes since birth: not because I did not want them but because I am a man who suffers many persections, as my wife will confirm. Give a free society based upon natural laws I would have my sons and daughters at my knee. Instead, it is the wish of governments and conspirators that the knee of Jean-Jacques should be given a baser occupation. To bend. To bend! My lords, I have a mortal aversion to any form of compulsion.

Happiness is quite indescribable. It can only be felt and the stronger the feeling the less it can be described. With unhappiness this is not the case. We can examine it and find its roots because our minds protest and demand explanations. I have constantly demanded a reason why I have not been able to enjoy a love of complete natural joy. My habit of masturbation is an equivocation, though justified in a philosopher: my penchant for physical pain during love-making can be explained through childhood experiences which I will come to shortly: but it does not satisfactorily answer the question – why cannot this man, who loves Nature, who loves womankind, fulfil his sexual promise to the absolute brim? I must turn your attention to society: to the way we are educated; the way we live.

This is my theme and if there is offence to be taken here tonight I will take it from a world that has ruined my potential and discoloured my vision of the Supreme Being, the most sexual, the most creative force we have in our midst.

I have committed crimes in my life: theft, betrayal, cruelty, and they need not concern us now as they are not the subject of my discourse. For these crimes I have suffered, usually by conscience rather than punishment as they were peccadilloes if the truth be told. There was a time when I was about nine when I was boarded out to be fostered by a pastor, Monsieur Lambercier, to study Latin and all the rubbish that masquerades as education. I was a lively boy but I do not believe that there has ever been a child with less vanity. I worked hard at my lessons but fell short of expectations and the pastor's sister resorted to physical chastisement. When I was thrashed I discovered that the experience of being beaten by a mature woman was not entirely unpleasurable and it came to pass that I would contrive mischief in order to be assailed by Mademoiselle Lambercier, with whom I fell in love.

The confusion that exists here between the law and sex is clear. The lack of care that the pastor took in determining the rightness of my punishment created a conundrum in my childish mind.

I have argued to myself on my long, lonely journeys into exile, that I have spent my life seeking the opprobrium of those set in authority because it gives me pleasure, not because I disapprove of their methods of government. However, it was a boy of nine who responded in that way. I was unafraid, excited, willing to be aroused by pain. If there is a lesson in later life it is surely that: to make use of pain and never waste suffering.

I should add that when the pastor himself beat me there was no pleasure in it at all. As Mademoiselle Lambercier became exhausted, or aware of my delight, she passed the responsibility for my chastisement increasingly to him. My response was to become better behaved so corporal punishment won the day, but it was a hollow victory. If the persecutions that I endure ever reach their ultimate stage and my life is forfeit I imagine that I will go to the gallows as a groom to the bridal bed.

Death to the lover of political pain is, in the words of Shakespeare, a consummation devoutly to be wished.

It is hardly surprising that a boy who has been through experiences of this nature should be a late developer; sex having provided so many obstacles and horrors. I was well beyond twenty and had lived in the house of the woman who was to take my virginity for five years before it actually happened. This was Madame de Warens, the best woman that ever lived. She was ten years my senior and always had my best interests at heart.

Indeed, she already had one lover who lived with us in the same house at Chambery – a quiet, studious, respectful man called Anet who adored her – so it can not have been because of any shortage of sexual excitement that she wanted me. The spur of her desire was undoubtedly the attention that I was receiving from other ladies in the district who were being very lavish in their praises of my wit and accomplishments. Fearing that I would be corrupted, Mamma – that is what I called her, which speaks for itself about our relationship – took me aside one day and told me that it was her intention to grant me her favours and, in her generosity, she gave me eight days to consider the matter.

I ask you to imagine those eight days and my state of mind. There was Anet, her lover, busy about the house. There was Mamma, serious, thoughtful – not her usual self, full of gaiety – and there was Jean-Jacques, dreamy, distracted. Those eight days dragged on and on, but I wanted them to go on for longer. I dreaded what I desired! In fact I spent much of the time trying to find excuses for avoiding the denouement.

Put yourself in my place. Give yourselves my youth, my ignorance, my intoxication with deep feelings, my strength, my devotion to this beautiful woman as her adopted son. Remember my age – twenty and some years – a time when a young man is hungry for the love of women above all else, burning to prove himself, inflamed with desire to be completely and utterly a man.

Add to this that I was only happy when I was with Mama. That I had been with her for five glorious years – perhaps the most contented in my miserable life – then you will be able to understand my nervousness. This promised paradise had the potential to destroy our existing happiness. Such wisdom from a youth! There are few people who will not recognise the workings of an intuitively sage nature here.

I loved this woman with great passion but for herself, not for my satisfaction. In her I sought happiness, not pleasure. She was sister, mother, friend: now, it seemed, for my own protection, she had to be mistress as well. But I loved her far too much to desire her. In these later years that is the clearest interpretation I can come to.

The day dawned when I had to deliver my answer. There was a moment of self-disgust as I contemplated sharing Mamma with another man. I prayed that it would not reduce my respect for her as I am a man of natural delicacy. I could not avoid the thought that the arrangement was unworthy of all three of us but it was what Mamma wanted. So, I consented. The interview was grave, as was our joint behaviour. We dined together, I read aloud to her for a while. Anet was dismissed to his room and Mamma led me to her chamber. Let it not be supposed that the ten or twelve years difference in our ages had started to show on her. For me she had not aged at all since the first day that we met.

Her figure had become a little fuller, otherwise it was the same eye, the same skin, the same breasts, the same shining fair hair, the same light-heartedness, the same silvery voice. I was afraid that I would not be master of myself. The sight of her would make it impossible for me to take the short journey to her side with impunity. Everything could be wrecked! Then I found myself in the arms of a woman, a woman I worshipped, and I wept. I tasted the pleasure but it did not make me happy. In my heart it was incest.

What was it to her? She was neither sad nor excited. Her mood was cool and caressing. Mama was not at all sensual and she had not taken me in order to gratify herself. She neither received sexual pleasure nor the bitter remorse that afflicted me then and every time that we were sexually united afterwards.

The doom of our love was sealed that day. All the future sadness and disruption can be attributed to Mamma's lack of judgement. She assumed that I would leave her for another woman unless she anchored me. How wrong she was. We would be together now, I believe, if it were not for her mistake. Poor, poor Mamma. Poor me. My only family had gone in that bed.

Bearing this tragedy in mind I ask you to be lenient in your judgement of my subsequent sexual activities. A separation had occurred in my mind. I would struggle to resolve this, to unite the divided parts of my feelings, but I would not succeed.

In many ways I am a man of my time, though I condemn the cruel artifice and unnaturalness of it. The people I admire are often beset with vices that I deplore but practice: and none is worse than the one I am about to describe. Youth, I adore: my passion for it increases more as I lose sight of my own. To deprave youth is to poison the stream of natural life: but I have done it and for the most abominable of reasons. Convenience and economy.

My taste in friends is for those more fortunate than I. To receive the approval and liking of those of higher rank and fortune than myself pleases me. I admire the beauty and style of the women and the power of the men. My sympathies are not with them. I hate what they stand for but love what they are. I will walk miles through all weathers to dine at a great house: not to dazzle the company with my wit – for I am an inadequate conversationalist if I have nothing to say – but merely to be there and observe wealth and leisure and gaiety at work among people of accomplishment.

I wish you now to recall my children and what I did with them. They are in foundling hospitals where they will be better taken care of than I could ever manage. Their companions are, in general, of less fortunate birth. They are the bastard of consortiums of wealthy gentlemen, men with a business eye who buy up the daughters of the poor and keep them as cheap mistresses to share. When a child is born the girl does not know who the father is.

It is a shared risk. Oh, there is a love-roster! It is very civilised. I know because I have done it.

It is a form of slavery and it is I, Jean-Jacques, philosopher!, who has besmirched himself with this commerce. But I am surprised if many of the Christian gentlemen listening to me tonight do not know exactly what I am talking about. The bastards of London are as great an army as those of Paris.

Suppress you disgust if you can. To condemn this trade is hardly worth your while, its vileness is so obvious. But we are not here for that purpose, but to scrutinise the truth and to ask how it was created. I am a philosopher and a teacher. There is no educated person in the Old or New World who has not heard of me or my views on government, morality and justice. Yet I am capable of this horrendous degradation of natural goodness – for what else can a twelve-year old girl be but good?

I do not look for beauty in love. Beauty in sexual matters is a drug that I crave. These children are ill-educated, if at all, and we entrepreneurs undertake to improve them while they are in concubinage to us. We teach them how to read and write, we dress them, we instruct them in the polite graces, we give them what society deems to be advantages. So lust and education are a partnership and our hypocrisy is creative.

When we have tired of the girl she leaves our employment a skilful person but a ruined soul, unnatural, spiritually deformed, her child torn from her breast. She becomes a void.

Pause.

A member of this society.

He becomes very agitated.

Excuse me, a void. I am part of this so my authority to speak cannot be questioned. I know what I have done and my remorse is great, but I can give no guarantee that I would not do it again should the craving make itself felt. The poison of our society works in these veins but for me my veins are as glass and I can see the rise and fall of all my impurities. What I ask myself above all is what will become of my army of children? What will they believe in, those children of infamy? As they peep over the walls of the foundling hospitals of Paris what do they think? Surely they cannot help but see the corruption that has created them. When they come of age and walk out of the gates they will not willingly run to join that ancient order of things: they will have dreamed dreams in their simple cots together and I fear that it must be a dream of blood. How does that strike you?

Pause.

Ah, at last! I have broken through. Your cold-hearted disdain has started to thaw and you see me in a fresh light. Yes, I stand here like a bear in a cage, all fetters and ferocity, a political wild animal in bondage, a beast with the feelings of Europe's dishonoured millions raging in his blood.

That is my nature, but by now you intelligent and educated people can read me like a book. All my arguments, my philosophy, my love of liberty, equality, fraternity are founded on my feelings. My feelings. My sexual adventures exist as a personal history that cannot be replicated but I wonder whether the pattern that they follow is common to us all. It is a story of disappointment, of blunder, of ignorance and ecstasy ruled by stupid reservations. But the source, the fountainhead of natural feeling, sexual and spiritual, is God within us, and that is a common sense that I, even I, Jean-Jacques Rousseau will admit to.

Between the spring of our feelings and the time when they run into the sea of ourselves at death there is pollution; untruth, fear, brutality, injustice – and those poisons are the practice of government. And our governments are based on the feelings of a few. I have given you an insight into mine. Would you want to be governed by them? By one man? By one king? Am I not a focus of all these poisons because I am alone? If my feelings are shared out and understood and embraced and not condemned will I not become more of a sacred instrument of Nature?

All poisons are diluted if they are poured into clean water. They become less toxic. The same, I believe, is true of social and political and personal poisons. Dilute them with the blessed water of natural feelings which we recognise in each other. Sex! Yes!

What is all the terror about? It is all so simple. We come from the same well, all of us.

I have not frightened you by telling the truth. There is no one here who finds me disgusting. We have found a bond within my peculiarities. The clanking of my chains has struck a responsive chord in the tinkling of your own fetters. But we are cut off here in this room. Our purpose is to be apart to ponder. Outside is the world waiting to reassume its grip on us.

So, I go out with my precious feelings into the dark night. London does not want to listen. Paris does not want to listen. Tonight I have a bed, I have a room, I have solitude within this city. I will ask myself before I go to sleep: Jean-Jaques, did you make any conquests this evening? Or are you just a stranger to everyone but yourself? Well, there is always the tail to talk to and it will wag.

One of the sweetest things about sex is that it induces a sleep for me that is without dreams. When I wake in the morning my mind is fresh and clear as if it had been swept out. That is when I dream, when I am awake.

Remember, hated English, your time with Jean-Jaques. We have been friends, haven't we? Who else could I tell such stories to? It is my guess that at this moment you might like to make me your king. Why not? You know more about me than you do about the one you've got. How I feel. How I work. My faults. My strengths.

My lords, gentlemen, fellows and members, I take my leave with a correction for old Socrates, a philosopher who has enjoyed more respect than any other on earth. He was too loose, or at least incomplete in his advice, 'Know thyself.' For a better mankind in a better world, he should have said, 'Know thy feelings and share them in unashamed equality.' Good night.

Exits.

The End.

CRATES ON BARRELS

Crates on Barrels was first performed on 11 September 1975 by Christopher Crooks for Paines Plough (the inaugural production of the company) at The Young Studio, Lyceum Theatre, Edinburgh at the 1975 Festival.

Crates was a disciple of the great Cynic philosopher, Diogenes (413–327 BC) who lived in Athens in a barrel, according to the biographer, Diogenes Laertius. Crates was the teacher of the first Stoic philosopher, Zeno of Citium, and was thus the point of transfer from Cynicism to Stoicism. Although less famous than his teacher or disciple Crates was popular in his day, exemplifying the Cynic's wish to play a role, using the world as a theatre and human life as a divine play which could present a vision of a perfectly disciplined happiness.

Being caught unawares by a freak storm as he was swimming along the rocky south coast of Menorca, the author took refuge in a sea-cave. To keep his mind off the waves crashing at the entrance, he imagined the arched roof of the cave as the barrel of Diogenes, and the swifts nesting there as the spirits of the old Cynic and his disciple, Crates.

A barrel on its side, securely wedged, one end facing the audience, the top removed. Enter CRATES at the trot holding two oranges and a small sack of grain in his teeth. Almost naked, he runs round the barrel with one orange raised in his left hand, the other orange being rotated around it. Dropping the grain at the mouth of the barrel, he addresses the audience.

CRATES: The sun going round the earth and the moon going round the sun? Or Crates going round in circles with his breakfast? No prizes for the winner.

He dives into the barrel with the grain and oranges. For a moment he mutters indistinguishable remarks, then bursts into laughter.

You noticed?

He turns to the audience and thrusts his head out.

Anyone notice my bruises? Since I go about almost naked they should be obvious. They (*He jerks a thumb over his shoulder at the interior of the barrel.*) noticed at once. Still sharp-eyed. They know when I've been beaten up. It all goes down in their mental ledger. The seventeenth time this year. The officers are getting more and more skilful though, leaving less evidence. They worked me over for an hour last night and it hardly shows. If I weren't of such a rugged constitution I'd look like a mosaic floor by now. What was that?

CRATES ducks his head back into the barrel, pauses, then laughs uproariously.

That's good, I like that.

Pokes his head out again.

One of them asked if a man recovering from a severe beating by the city officers was the best person to give people advice on the pursuit of happiness? Are there as many gaps in my philosophy as there are in my teeth? A man must live, even a third-rate philosopher who is persecuted far above his abilities. I am discredited, I have no answers, all I offer is amusement, but they still want my blood. Isn't it ridiculous? A mere pavement artist like me treated as though I were a professional revolutionary. Today they may let up. Today they might decide that I am only a joke after all. Let's hope so.

Swings his legs out and sits cross-legged in the barrel opening.

Lovely day, warm, sunny. Mmmm. Yes, you'd be better off out here than carping away in the back there. Here they come, the masses, hoping to see the fun. Good crowd today, better than yesterday! The word must have got around about yesterday's fireworks. The officers dragged me away by force just as I was about to define decency. You all heard about that? Of course. That's why you're here. My friends in the back think it's all far too dramatic and not much to do with the truth.

Jumps up.

Crates, at your service, professional philosopher. I can teach you how to be happy, yes, happy. Roll up! Get happy quick with Crates! Come to the actual barrel of Diogenes and hear his disciple expound the wisdom of centuries. Only five minas! A bargain offer! Come forward, don't hang about at the back. Ah, I see my old comrades the spies from the chief officer. Give yourselves a clear exit men, but wait to hear the whole argument, eh? No running off in mid-sentence bellowing heresy or sedition. *Ah,* you're all smiling now. All the components are here, flint and steel. I cannot promise a violent sideshow, or a martyrdom, but there is a good chance. Take a gamble. Stay anyway. Perhaps the philosopher has something worth hearing? You may laugh sir, you may laugh.

CRATES leans against the barrel, holds up a hand.

Silence. Silence in there as well. Citizens, though never as great a man as my master Diogenes, I do one thing as well as he ever did. I am very good at beginning at the beginning.

Pats the barrel.

Your mother. See this tub as your mother. Some of you will need less imagination than others.

Points at himself.

Me? Your father, probably in wine after a jolly evening at the tavern.

Climbs on top of the barrel and simulates copulation, grunting.

Aaaaaaah! Pleasure! Godlike, the pleasure of creation. Oooooh, wonderful. The first of all pleasures.

Slides down off the barrel, picks up an orange out of the barrel and starts peeling it, sticking his thumb in.

You are conceived. Things start to happen. Outside there are planets, stars, thunderstorms and portents. Can these have an effect on you, Mister One In A Million?

Starts to eat the segments of orange, one by one.

You take shape. A big head, supposedly containing a brain. Arms. Legs. A nose. Eyes. Ears. Internal organs. There should be a heart somewhere. Spleen. Definitely an anus, oh yes, there must be an anus. Miles and miles of intestine. The seeds of teeth. And instincts. Ah, instincts. You grow, hunched up in the barrel of your mother's belly, an expanding dwarf.

Gets into the barrel and kneels on all fours, facing audience.

The magic moment. Waiting to be born. It is all out there. Mmmm, muscles working on either side of your great skull, contractions, the old lady working up a storm. Mmmm, not long. Here we go!

Crawls out of the barrel painfully, writhing.

Aaaaaaah! Being born! Being born! Here!

Stands up, spreads his arms.

There! All over. (*Looks over his shoulder at the barrel.*) All right in there, I know that I have left many questions aside but I have not much time. One of the spies is already twitching. Yes Heraclitus, we will get down to discussing earth air fire and water, next week if I'm still here. (*Turning back to the audience.*) So we have a new arrival. While all that process was taking place something else was growing, or at least being planted. (*Pause.*) No, you can't tell me. You savages are only here for the sport. What faces. What ugly faces. What instinct. to pay money to see me hounded from pillar to post. You disgust me. I am talking about the soul of this new-born creature, the soul. Here it is.

Cups his hands.

What changes this pure thing into the muddy and stinking corruption that you are? Who violates it? It should be me who comes to see you beaten, all of you. I would pay with my life to see you flogged by those same officers who abuse me. You are contemptible. Why are you here? Go home, go on, leave me with this boy, this handful of virtue. If you breathe on him he will die. What a vile population of gogglers and consumers, mouths and members, ugh, come lad, don't look at them.

Pause, CRATES walks angrily forward, thrusting out his cupped hands.

How would you train him? What would you train him for? (*Mumbles.*) Yeh, well, ah, hm, first thing is… War!

Vaults onto the barrel and rides like a horse.

Remember Marathon! Remember Salamis! Athens for ever! Death or glory! Hack them to pieces! (*Pause, he sits back.*) As soon as our boy is able to walk, this is the good you would teach him. You appal me! He was born a citizen of the universe and you teach him to be a murderer in the pay of one squalid Greek town! How dare you bend that boy so! Mean and greedy arrogance! What bloodthirsty creatures you are.

CRATES peers down into the barrel through the bung-hole.

All right Hercules. Don't get upset just because I abuse Athens, I think you soldiered for God, not one town. Patriotism is an evil. It blinds us. It cripples our minds. Hercules, you know that Cyrus the Persian was the enemy of Athens, yet he was a philosopher of great insight. A loyal Athenian would be forced to say that he was only a barbarian and grant him no credit as a thinker. That's stupid, isn't it? Of course it is. And my old master Diogenes agrees with me. When he was asked which city he came from he always answered 'the city of the universe'. No, no, you argue it out with my master then.

CRATES smiles at the audience.

The way the military protect each other is marvellous isn't it? Poor Hercules, he has the old soldier's affliction, nostalgia. War is joy.

Shouts down the bung-hole.

Cyrus the Persian did not say we should enjoy suffering! Shut up for a moment.

He slides off the barrel.

To get back to this boy. What are we going to teach him? Follow me now, step by step.
What is taught?
Knowledge is taught.
What is knowledge?
Socrates said virtue was knowledge.
So virtue can be taught?

Certainly.
Socrates also said, know thyself. Did he mean virtue
thyself?
No, he meant that by finding self-knowledge you would
find virtue. Was he meaning that the virtue was already
implanted there, at birth?

Pause, CRATES looks at the barrel, waits.

That is not what he said.
But is it what he implied?

Pause, CRATES looks at the barrel again. Waits. Shrugs.

A new approach then.
Can self-knowledge be taught?
Only self can know self.
But the method? How to do it?
And while we're about it, does
Our handful have an hereditary human virtue?

Pause. CRATES leans over and peers into the barrel.

Well Socrates, aren't you saying anything? This time I've
tied you in knots.

CRATES stands up, triumphant and rattles off his next proof.

How can self Alpha
Teach self Beta
Anything but Alphaism?

CRATES freezes in mid-skip and stands to attention.

Yes master. I'm sorry master. I did not know that
Socrates was having a nap, or that you had got back.
How was your journey? I will correct the misimpression
with my students.

CRATES returns to audience.

A moment of light relief. The point is, self can be *trained*
by a system developed by Diogenes. You will all
remember the true story of how my master, when

captured by pirates, set about retraining their souls? Even when they sold him into slavery, the course only being partly successful, he answered the question of a prospective buyer as to what skills he had by saying, 'I am good at governing men.' The man did not make the purchase and is it any wonder my master was afterwards set at liberty?

Pause, CRATES glances slyly at the barrel.

My sincerity is trustworthy. As was my master's when caught helping his father to counterfeit coins. It was, he suggested, merely a symbolic art to illustrate his rejection of conventional morality. But the system, the system. We Cynics believe in poverty. Give everything you have away, but not to the poor as that would spoil their grace, but to the already-rich. Give them more so they choke. Strip yourself down to these essentials. Go naked.

Puts his hand on his chest.

Yourself. Maybe a rough cloak for cold days. Maybe a staff to lean on while climbing mountains. Maybe a cloth to cover the demon.

Leans on the barrel, grinning.

Try to stay as pure as the day you came into the world. The boy? The handful? The same. Give him nothing. Make him want nothing.
If you want nothing
And you get nothing
You must be happy
For you have got what you want.

Steps away from the barrel, giving it a bang.

Aha, that woke Socrates up. A false proof is all the prodding he needs. Of course, of course, what we must cure is the wanting, even wanting nothing. Yes, we must crush desire. (*Pause.*) So how do we desire virtue? (*Pause.*)

39

Got you! You have no answer! Desire must stay. How would I get an audience if there was no desire? Right now I can count five men known to me who are aflame with desire for the Good – each one wants to be the first back to the chief officer with news of my overstepping the mark yet again. The mark is good. The chief officer is good. The news will be good. You will get what you want. I will get what I want which is publicity. Let me bring this good closer. The Delphic Oracle is a loathsome confidence trick which thrives on mindless superstition and the idiocy of its patrons. The priestesses are exhausted harlots doing part-time work and munching the sacred bay leaves with the same enthusiasm as goats chew nettles. Got all that? The Delphic Oracle is a foul sham. The Delphic Oracle is poisonous. Any man who believes that it has divine powers would also give credence to the story that all wisdom emanates from the arseholes of farmhorses. You see? I *desire* to destroy not only myself, but the Delphic Oracle. I would gladly see all your conventions in ruins, including the one whereby impoverished philosophers have to die to prove the plainest point. The spies are hovering. Are you coming or going? Will I say something worse while you are gone? Let us get back to our boy. Come, come lad, hold my hand. Naked, brimming with virtue inside. What a struggle it is to get that virtue outside where we can all see it. Don't look at them. There is not an atom of virtue in them, not a tiny speck. They are well-used, dirty, fatigued, past redemption. Inside my barrel? Ah, a different proposition. Isn't that right masters? Philosophy's job is to achieve happiness by choosing the right efforts, efforts which conform to Nature. I have a barrelful of natural men, heroes of Nature. You are doubtful boy? Sceptical? Tut.

Leans down as if talking face to face with child.

Aaaah. (*Holds his groin.*) Ooh, sorry. Phew, I'm feeling a few after-effects. They know where to press home their arguments, those officers. I'll have to sit down for a moment...hold on...poor body eh, poor resistance... oof...

He slowly lowers himself to the ground and leans against the barrel.

Ah, that's better. Strange the tactics they use. You would think that as they were beating up a philosopher they'd go for his most valuable equipment – the head. But they don't, perverse creatures that they are. They treat me as if I was a rapist or an adulterer – neither of which I am. It would be a great help to philosophy if its exponents could develop some kind of defence against these attacks. Maybe, like most animals, the genital organs could be carried inside the body? Or all philosophers be castrated at birth? But how would we know them? That would be the surest way of all parents turning completely against our trade. Phew, they don't hold back. Do you know the pain? It surges, then dies away, surges, makes you want to be sick. Now the head is a different matter. All bone like an old war-club. Tonight I will offer them my head. Please use my head tonight I'll say, Have a go at that instead...providing they will agree to leave my tongue unharmed. I'll need my tongue for tomorrow won't I? We must continue with the course. How can I possibly teach you to be happy if I am dumb? I suppose I could draw pictures in the dust with a stick. That wouldn't be the same though and I'm no artist. Ah, I feel better. The pain has gone away again. Yes, I'll get back on my feet so you can see at the back. Here we go.

He drags himself on the barrel, stands upright, flexes himself, then grins.

Right as rain by the time they start again. I have worked it out that I must recover from one beating before they start on another, otherwise the effects will accumulate and I will go under. It is a matter of self-control and discipline. Right now my head is saying to my organs of reproduction – settle down, it never happened. You imagined it all. You are in fine fettle and the city officers never came near you yesterday. In fact, I could probably persuade my organs of reproduction that the city officers do not even exist! Why should they? To me they have no sexual interest – none whatsoever – ah, a flaw, I could want to use a city officer as a urinal as a repayment for having a vessel of the chief officer's piss forced down my throat on one occasion. No, vengeance is not an emotion I must encourage in myself. The chief officer was only doing his job. He is, to say the very least, a vineyard of a man. Oh dear, my poor lad. He is shocked. I forget about him. Perhaps I should have kept this kind of autobiographical detail for an exclusively adult audience. You're right boy, back to happiness, back to my task. Let me put before you the greatest philosophical statement ever made, to my mind. Antisthenes, the founder of Cynicism by many accounts, said that he would rather be a madman than experience pleasure. So pleasure as a way to happiness is right out. Oho, you do look disappointed. You didn't realise that it wasn't that easy, did you? All those little moments of contentment, success, satisfaction, all meaningless. No, you must go naked in the rain, barefoot in the snow, exposed in the burning sun. Why don't you all get up and go home? Not one of you has any intention of following our advice. You think we Cynics are madman. Old Antisthenes was quite wrong. He had no choice between being a madman and experiencing pleasure, because he was already a madman and could not experience pleasure, except the pleasures of the mad. And what are they? Going naked in the rain, barefoot in the snow...so what I am telling you to do is to accept a new definition of pleasure. Take yours, examine it, then accept its exact opposite as pleasure and your original concept as pain. In that way a good dinner is nauseating, a fine wine poisonous, your house a pig-sty. Look at it that way and you'll come out here and live with me. We'll squat in the middle of our magnificent city, an army of paupers, accusing, accusing. Will the officers be able to treat all of us as they treat me? No, for they will be here as well, having rejected Athens and all her material pretensions. Man, and the improvement of Man will be our new city. We will train ourselves towards a true and indestructible virtue based on an intelligent happiness…won't we? Hmm? The boy is agitated. He says I've left something out. I'm not giving the full story…

He snaps his fingers.

That's what's missing. I forgot to bring in God. How could I forget God? Go and sit down again lad. We must deal with God. I have a barrelful of men who are intimate with the deity. Speak up in there! Where does our boy stand with regard to God?

Pause. CRATES cocks a hand to his ear.

Come on. I'm waiting. I expected a thunder of replies. I'm ready to reel, deafened.

CRATES kneels and peers into the barrel.

Is there not one of you who is willing to help us out? What about you Hercules? Can't you give us an insight into your father? Who can? It's a wise son who knows his own father. Blasphemy. Careful. Don't carry that back to the city officers. I must talk about God though if we are to get anywhere this morning. Who else should I ask for help but blind Homer? He is in there, joined at the head and hip to his creation, Ulysses, half-truth, half-lie, half-poem, half-fact, half-history, all God, gods everywhere, multitudes of gods. Now it is getting crowded in there. I am still not confused. Antisthenes, you recall that off-hand remark of yours that to avoid being corrupted a wise man should not learn to read? I hope you are sitting next to Homer. Let us proceed with God, or gods as they do have a tendency to multiply. Or should that be He has a tendency to multiply being self-procreating, therefore creating knowledge which might be virtue? Is changing yourself into a bull to couple with a nubile girl an act of virtue? Rubbish, non-thinking rubbish. We will cast that aside. By agreement? Any dissenters? If God is the maker of virtue then he cannot also be a witless and bestial fornicator. Or am I presuming? Is there more than one side to God's nature and is one of them *unnatural*? Can God be unnatural? If not then it may be virtuous for me to grab the nearest goat and service it at the high altar before the whole congregation of pious Athenians. Would they applaud? Well done son! Encore! What are we dealing with? Our boy rejects these visions. No one in Greece has seen God. We do not know what we are talking about. We do not know if there is a God. Oops, heresy. Don't tell anyone I said that. Tell the spies to resume their places. Of course we know that there is a God, but we do not know what He is like. That pompous bore Plato said that all men seek the good by nature and that God sustains the order of Nature, but is human nature therefore the Nature of God? What is that man saying? That we all have a piece of God in us? Ah, I see the spies are leaving again. I recant immediately. Let us, for the moment, put God in with his worthies. God, I put you in the barrel with some of your old comrades. Is that agreed? If I am to get on I must put God aside with earth air fire and water – and get back to that boy. Where is he? Sitting there, quiet, well-behaved, and naked, wondering what this is all about. He is now watching God as he gets into the barrel on his hands and knees. An impressive sight from the back. Ah, I have a chance to clear up the mess which God may have made in your minds. He is not here. I am here, the boy is here, you are here, even the spies have remained behind, totting up my mistakes. We start with a clean sheet, well, not quite. A few jottings perhaps.

CRATES beckons to the imagined boy.

In the absence of God I will discuss power. See.

CRATES sits on the barrel.

A king. We will say, a tyrant. Absolute power. Kneel boy. Kneel. You can get away with not kneeling to God, but not to a tyrant. You must kneel. There is no point in not doing so. Yet all of you know the story of the day that Alexander the Great came to visit my master Diogenes. The king asked him if there was any favour that he could grant him. Diogenes, who was sunbathing at the time, merely asked him if he would be so good as to take his shadow elsewhere. And the great king did so and afterwards confessed that if he was not himself, emperor of the world, he would want to be Diogenes, a poor, naked philosopher. Why did Alexander then kneel before Diogenes? How was the process reversed, this natural political process? Why did fear not produce servility? If any of you know the answer then you can go home for I can teach you nothing.

CRATES slowly gets down from the barrel.

I would have my boy grow up to look the tyrant in the eye and speak his mind. No matter how obscenely cruel, how foul in temper, how mad or disgusting, my boy here will tell the man of power what he honestly thinks of him. That is the ultimate test of his training, the proof of his happiness. A wise valour. An intelligent courage. How do I create this in you? Are you worth it? Have I changed your idea of happiness too much? I have taken away your wine, your flowers and left you staring at death, quite defenceless. Or are you armed?

He looks at the barrel.

They are all quiet now, listening to see if I get it right. (*Pause.*) There is one law that has never been observed. It has always been there, but never obeyed. It states that because we are animal, because we suffer from the agony of greed, the only man who is fit to govern over us should be materially worthless, a man in whom the urge

45

for wealth is totally dead after years of disciplined suppression. Our tyrant should be a beggar. His ambition to get poorer. His lust, for the good of all.

CRATES pauses, stares at the audience.

Well? Come on, someone say it. Where's a practical man? It's impossible isn't it? Or course it is. It would reverse all the natural trends in society. We are an acquisitive species. The best of us is the most successful accumulator. It is the rich who rule the earth, quite right too. They're the ones with initiative, energy; drive. What an idea. To have a beggar in a seat of government. So we must teach our boy hunger. He must hunger. He must aspire, be a collector. Clothe him at once. Dazzle him. Discredit the Cynics and their supreme invention, Liberty, and give the lad *your* objectives. Things are fine as they are. Here in Athens we rub along, democrats one day, slaves the next, a war here, war there, few rebellions, famines, but we get through. We survive. Isn't that the most natural instinct of all? Isn't virtue survival? (*Pause.*) Complete silence from the back. My friends the informers stand rooted to the spot, amazed by my conclusions. Now they're off! The spell has broken. That was heresy! Ah, at the rear I see my colleague Aristotle shaking his head. He has witnessed a terrible betrayal. For I am handing over our handful to you, the people, to bring up. Surely your instincts are surer than mine? Go to them boy, go on. (*Pause.*) He is hesitating. Why? (*Pause.*) Is it that he senses who is the happier man? If not then I would be paying the mob to teach me and what could I learn? We Cynics are the spokesmen of the workers of Greece, yet they reject us. Behind me I have a barrelful of aristocrats of the mind, the mind of course, and they are dead, at least transfigured. They are critical of me because I have a poor brain when compared to their laden skulls. Yet our boy clings to me. See, I have his hand. Even with the city officers on their way to shut me up, I have his hand. He takes me seriously. He loves me. I love him. He loves me as I loved Diogenes and as he loved Antisthenes and he loved Socrates and all the way back to the great Hercules who loved God and was his son. What a company we are, so stretched out over Time. And all this *love*. Who brought that up? How can we Cynics who observe and spy on Man's corrupt desires, talk about love when we are so sneaky? What's that boy?

CRATES laughs and pats the boy's head.

Yes lad, I had worked that out for myself. He tells me that the spies will have got back to the chief officer by now and I only have a few minutes left. It is all very sad. When is the chief officer going to find some reasonable hirelings who appreciate my finer points? They always prosecute me for my more ridiculous assertions and outbursts, never for the good stuff. They'll do me for the Delphic Oracle today and I've said all that a thousand times. Now what he should thrash me for is my passion for hypocrites. I adore hypocrites. I would suffer for hypocrites. What we need is an acceptable system of insincerity. No I'll change that. What *we* have got is an acceptable system of insincerity, and it works. We stagger on. The city manages one way or another. What's that?

Listens at the bung-hole and laughs.

Socrates says that things are not what they used to be. He was never beaten, only executed, and he hated hypocrites. What I would criticise is the system whereby the officers arrest me, call me sir, then thrash me when I would rather be called pig and dealt with decently. That is hypocrisy taken to the lengths of perversion. It is enough that honesty has become dishonesty, that the elected politician is there to ruin you and the frustrated and envious assassin your only friend, that wisdom and strength belong solely to the cretin and love is the secret vice of the city executioner. Yes, see them turning the corner into the square? Going on past experience I know they'll give me a few more minutes – hello there – you see, it's to give me more rope to hang myself – yes, they're assembled. The anti-Crates squad is now all ears.

Listens at the bung-hole.

What a welter of advice. They are so confused. Hercules wants me to defend myself like a man. Ulysses recommends a ploy, feigning illness. Socrates suggests good-humoured acceptance, Heraclitus...well, Heraclitus wants to know when I'm going to discuss his theory of the elements...not with the officers I think. I've tried that and got my bollocks truncheoned for trying. Hmmm, oh dear, trouble...chief officer is there himself. That's bad. Serious. I'm in for it this time. What is it lad? The old folk? He says that there is an uproar behind. They are all shouting at me.

CRATES bangs the barrel several times.

Quiet in there! Quiet! Pick a spokesman.

He covers up his ears, laughing.

That put the cat amongst the pigeons. I can hear Hercules booming away and Socrates being very pithy...is that Ulysses singing a sea-shanty to Homer's harp accompaniment? Who have you elected? Who is fittest to speak? I should have thought! God of course. With a minority report from Plato? How did he slither in? What does God say?

Pause. CRATES presses his ear to the barrel.

Same old stuff. God says God is Love but Plato says God is just a good organiser. Master, Diogenes, haven't you got a word of wisdom for these assembled fools? Ah, that's more like it. He says, 'The sage will love for only the sage knows we must love.' Care to define 'love' master? Not today. So we have a new concept. Now, is this useful philosophical term love already instilled in

our handful, the boy? If I say love to him will he sparkle
with recognition or just yawn? When facing the tyrant,
will it be useful? Diogenes says yes, it will help to set an
example. God says yes as it always acts as an anaesthetic
if you have to suffer the pains of death. Is this the second
great unobserved law then? Are you all agreed?

CRATES leaves the barrel, radiant.

So we have it! Number Two. If Number One Neglected
Law is that the poor must rule, Number Two is that all
men must love. We'll drill that into our boy…with love
of course. Even from this distance I can hear Hercules
bellowing a question: what do we do with the man who
refuses to love? He says cut off his head. God tends to
agree. Antisthenes says it is impossible, Plato reckons
that all men naturally love as loving is choosing the
good and we all do that instinctively…don't we? I mean,
when the officers get hold of me round the back of the
court I'll be able to see their Platonic instincts at close
quarters won't I? My answer to Hercules that I must love
such officers in particular so they may be persuaded to
love me, though I have to confess to doubt. Many
women have found me unlovable, even my own mother.
I know for sure that not one of the officers loves me.
How do I tell this boy of ours that I am going to commit
suicide by trying to do the impossible?

Mimes picking up the boy and sitting him on the barrel.

We will say he, this innocent lad, is the chief officer. I
know he hates me. He has broken up my tutorials a
thousand times, threatened my person, and my life.
Within an hour I will be in his room again, accused of
heresy. He knows what I think of his God, his
pretensions and his Law. What am I worth to the state? If
any of you found me lying in the Porch of Zeus
tomorrow with my head kicked in, you would step over
me and hurry on your way. Socrates shouts that I'm
right. So you would. So what stops the chief officer from

killing me? It is not because the poor rule Athens, for they patently do not – nor is it that mean do love – which they evidently cannot find the spirit to – so what is it keeps me alive?

CRATES grins and lifts the boy down.

Time. The chief officer has the power of pain over me. He can put me to death. But he cannot put me out of memory. I do not say that death is of no consequence – a chorus of wholehearted agreement from the back there – but I do say that a strong and virtuous self which observes the two unobserved laws, can cheat death. The self will live. Who has not heard of Socrates? Who will remember the chief officer? In a hundred years it will be possible for Man to be governed honestly because of Time, the third but observed law, will bring all the memories of our virtuous men together and the force of that memory will be irresistible. It will scrape every corrupt king from his throne, every criminal from his hideaway, every chief officer from his chambers. Our heroes, my friends, my masters, will bring about that change. Hercules, Ulysses, Homer, Heraclitus, Antisthenes, Socrates, Diogenes the dog, even tedious Plato – the new age will be born from them. Reason, love, hard work, training, poverty…ah, all the good things in life will come into their own. We Cynics, now more abused than beggars, without a city, without a house or country, the truly poor who shelter in public places and eat the scraps from your tables, we will rule the world for you. (*Pause.*) Ah, a spot of rain. You are restless. I think that's all for today. All over. Will anyone come with me to the interrogation to act as my witness? Your five minas will be repaid for the service. No? I have made progress this morning. Wait for me then, we will all leave together. I must have my arguments in hand. Hold on while I liberate my masters and release God. Stand back boy, he comes out like an enraged elephant. Oh dear, the chief officer has had enough. He's very angry. I can smell the officers already. Is this it? Will they kill me this time? Is this my last day? What a life. That's all. I'm finished.

CRATES crawls into barrel, then reappears with a cage full of small birds. He holds out a hand for the boy. The birds flutter about and whistle. CRATES holds up the cage.

Here they are. Aren't they beautiful? I love that streak of yellow down the back of Hercules. The daylight is too bright eh? Blinking away, blinded, look at them, poor things. God ate quite a lot of your breakfast eh? All right, let's get on with it. Try the head today if you will. The head.

CRATES exits clutching the cage to his chest.

Ends.

LATER

Later was first performed at The King's Head, Islington, London, on 4 June 1979 by Mary Ellen Ray for Paines Plough, directed by herself.

Russia, 1937. In a small village near Novgorod, a family, many of whose children have been lost or are missing in the turmoil of the Revolution and its aftermath, try to make contact with their loved ones. Sonia, the eldest daughter, returns. She has been away for sixteen years but has answered the call to come home and help her family get out of trouble.

Later was written in 1979 following a research trip to the USSR for the play *Master Class*. While travelling from Moscow to Leningrad overnight the train got stuck in a snowdrift. Outside, in sub-zero temperatures, a woman worked, shovelling snow from under the train. She looked through the carriage window at which Pownall was sitting. It was this moment, joined to the presence of Mary Ellen Ray at his side, that inspired the writing of the play.

Darkness. Amplified sound of a glass sliding over a table top. Amplified voice of a woman spells out S-O-N-I-A synchronised with the sound of the glass. A light starts to grow, revealing a shawled figure standing behind an old wooden chair. Her voice reduces to normal levels.

SONIA: Sonia. Yes, it's me. No! Don't get up! Give me time to get my breath back. Quiet now. Don't be frightened. You asked me to come, and I'm here. I hurried before you changed your minds. Please don't move. I must have a moment to establish myself. What a ride! I'm still breathless with the speed of it. See how the frost is melting in my hair. Mamushka, raise your eyes again. It is me. See how I'm still the same. You summoned me, didn't you? You called for me just like you used to do from the back door when I was working in the garden. Sonia! Sonia! It hurts the eyes, travelling so fast and so far, but the pain is going as I look at you all again – my family. My family. Ooh! Don't scratch the table-top. I spent enough time polishing it to care. I know. Your hands are trembling. Wait. Make them strong and steady.

Pause.

There, we can go on. No. Change the glass. That one has a chip in it. Get another one from the sideboard, father.

Pause.

That's better. The other one was making me wince every time it got near a crack. There are enough marks on that table, eh Mamushka? Everyone has left a sign there at some time. Alexi feels sick. I know that tinge of his around the gills. Swallow hard Alexi! Count up to fifty. That's how we used to do it. Aren't your hearts beating fast? I can hear them from here. They sound like a herd of horses. It's so cold. Twenty below outside. What a darkness I whirled through. I couldn't tell which was star and which was snow. But you're warm in here. Who pushed you to get that beautiful new stove? Me. It was a good buy. You must bless my name every time you get up in the morning. There is worse weather coming down from north. I passed through it over the Baltic. I could not see the earth at all. Ssssh. I'm nearly settled now. I think the dog should go out. It cannot understand. He can see me, but I have no scent. Go on, take him out. Open the door as little as you can. Is the light on in the sitting-room? No. I love light but this is no time for it. No, you can't touch. I said no, Mamushka! You will spoil everything. My presence here hangs on a thread. You believe this is Sonia. Don't try and prove it with your hands. You will find nothing, nothing. Sit down again, back round the table. There are little rules which govern this appearance. Why not obey them so I can enjoy my visit? Most of you were laughing when you came into the room to ask for Sonia to come back. You did it for Mamushka, to please her. Well, I am doing it for Sonia, to please her, to amuse her. Have you ever thought how flat and grey it is where I am? You're crying Mamushka. It's been a long time since I saw a tear. You will see through the glasses of your tears again. I have, many times. All I did and did not. I can see the paper patterns I left in my drawer, but I cannot hold the scissors now. My fingers are holes themselves. You do not understand. How do you think Christ clung to his cross? Not by nails, but through the holes the nails made. That is how I cling to life. There is no terror, but I have not been purged. I don't escape what I have done. That is what keeps me in orbit – which, officially, is where I am – in an orbit so long that it feels flat and grey. It is not good, it is not bad by your standards.

Laughs.

We should celebrate! This is the first time that this family has achieved anything unusual. In this comfortable fug in here with your faces shining, I can remember hours and hours of torpor. We sat and stared at each other until the spring came. Vodka stripped your nerves down to the last thin wire, my father, and there were evenings when you screamed aloud and went out into the snow to curse the way the seasons worked. Such boredom, family, such indolence, such apathy! The Christians are right. Life is a preparation for death. Open the stove for me so I can see the centre of the earth again. That was my favourite story, father, and you always told it well. Why was your school always such a cold and rigid place when that thought, our stove, boiled at the back of your mind?

Pause.

It wasn't so bad after all. Imagination is a terrible thing and I know what hell you must have gone through, but believe me, Death isn't as bad as it's painted. I would rather have been at home when it happened, however, here I am anyway. The circumstances are different. I'm here, you're there, there's this space in-between, but at least we're in touch again. Before we go any further, I'm sorry. I should have told you. You would have helped me, I know that. Going off on my own to sort it out was stupid when I had you both to give a hand. Having had time to think about it I can see that I was in too much of a hurry, didn't want to waste time, didn't want the burden of it right then when so much was happening in my life, so I thought, get rid. Have it removed and do it sensibly, practically, don't feel about it. Keep that for later. Now it makes me smile. My life was half over and I was thinking of later. When would I have had that child? And you were so eager to be old, old grandparents. With everything that was being torn up and changed around you, I sympathized with that. It would have been an anchor for you. Instead, I went to Petrograd. Selfish. Stupid. You would think that I had all that great movement in my bones, that as I walked along the street I shifted the world with me – it was absolutely selfish and self-centred. I was one woman and the only thing I could do to the required standard was work a sewing machine. But they did look smart, my uniforms. I was in all of them, wandering about, saluting, shouting. It was me looking out of all the button-holes, and my mind was being stretched. It was so exciting, even in that room in Novgorod with all the others, measuring great men across the shoulders...

Pause.

This will have to be kept a secret. Don't let anyone here talk about what we're doing or there will be trouble. For one thing the authorities won't accept the validity of this meeting, and for another they will accuse you all of promoting primitive superstition. Christianity is bad enough but this...

Pause.

It took you long enough to get round to it. Not that I have been waiting for the call, but I knew you were desperate. Not knowing must have been the worst part of it. I gave a false name to the man who did it and when it happened to go wrong he just dumped me as best he could and said nothing. I disappeared. He stuck me and the baby, what there was of it into a tin box with a pile of bricks and slid us into the river. We're still there, the matter anyway. You keep some kind of connection but the distance is colossal. It is like a needle-hole in cloth. Now I'm the cloth and the matter, the tin trunk, is the needle-hole. I'm all round it, and the hole is through me, but it lies at a distance that only an astronomer could talk about and make sense, yet it has nothing to do with stars, space, it is still within the known experience of life that we exist, me and Stefan. He was a boy. Everything he had was correct and well-balanced. If he had been born he would have been a perfect child but in his shape here he is only half-realized. To bring him here tonight would have been cruel on you because you would have been frightened. He wouldn't have turned a hair.

Pause.

I think you had guessed, Ma. The man was someone I met in the fitting-room. He was a good ten years

younger than me and I could hardly get the tape-
measure across his back. You might have met him, I
can't remember. There was so much coming and going
in those days, so many people. Novgorod was one thing,
the way it came to life and filled up after the civil war,
even with the famine, but Petrograd! You have never
seen so many people. They seemed to be walking on
each others heads along the pavements, taller than the
palaces, thicker than flies.

Pause.

There's someone coming. Nobody move. Ssssh. They'll
think you are out if you don't make a sound. Don't touch
the curtains. It's Dmitri from next door. He'll want to
borrow something. Let him get well away. He had a
good nose around. Not a bad sort, but nosey. You see,
he'd tell on you, not knowing what damage he was
doing. They were sitting in the dark, the whole family,
with one glass in front of them. One glass! Dmitri would
find that hard to believe unless it held ten gallons and
was filled with vodka. Am I going too fast for you?
What a rumble it makes, sliding across the table, and
you see me through letters. I exist in the alphabet. Let
me know if you get tired. One word takes so long. If
Time was not elastic for me, I'd fall asleep while you
were spelling out Russia. R–U–S–S–I–A. To you it is so
slow, to me, so quick. Like your old concertina, Boris.

Laughs.

Everything I've missed. All the effort I took to be in the
middle of it all, not understanding a tenth of what was
going on, and I was ambushed. No, Mamushka, I don't
want to answer questions. That is not the way it works.
I'm not accountable. No! The code you used works this
way – Sonia, have you got anything to say to us? You
ask me if I have anything to say, but I do not ask you. I
know what you have to say. It is not worth listening to
because it flies out of terror and unhappiness and is not
straightforward. You are talking to the dead, so you are

hysterical, emotional. I am talking to the living, so I can be natural. I am the natural. The state you are in makes any question, any demand you make, a waste of time. It is all too much for you. Quieten down now. I am not coming back. This is all you will have. You will not be able to share it with anyone but the people who sit in this is room – the family. If you will take my advice, never even talk about it. Go to Petrograd, put on your best clothes if you like, buy some flowers, throw them in the River Neva somewhere near the fortress. That will be near enough. Then lock your tongue on my name. It is only your stubbornness that is making you argue with me – as you used to when we chewed over politics – yes, how could I think this, how could I think that...now it's, now can I be here? About death, there is only a minute's worth of pity – you'll know – but about my life, about why I threw all my time away sewing uniforms for big boys with brilliant banners – that prompted months of anger, didn't it? Why did I court so much trouble when I was only half-aware of what it was all about? Working for nothing, playing dangerous games, was it the danger that upset you or having to shift for yourselves? Mamushka, I was a mother by the time I was eight, bringing up your children. Sonia, wash the girls, Sonia, give us our breakfast, Sonia, I need new trousers for the boys: there is the material... I had had nine children of yours by the time I shared a room with a man and got his child going. Any wonder I wanted to live my own life? Is it surprising I offered my needle to an army? All my dolls had blood in their veins, Mamushka. My child was given away in the same spirit, a doll to death, but it turned and bit me. No, Mamushka, I am not blaming you. I know I could have come home and had the child – you would not have turned your back on me, none of you would have done that. But I knew that if I came home, and it was born, I would never get away again. Me in the kitchen. Me in the garden. Me and this old house becoming the same thing. But I knew that you would never have let me down. And I did think of you in that room.

Pause.

After I'd lost an hour's steady flow of blood I knew I was going. The quack made himself scarce and locked the door. I couldn't move because he'd tied me down to the bed. I told myself that it was enough to live for the Party and to die by accident, that was what happened to lost people. There was no drama, no speech from the scaffold, nothing but weakness, tiredness, sleep, out. I had a clear conscience about others, including you, for I'd given the family all I had and always done my duty, but suddenly I felt angry. It made me mad, lying there in that mess, floating in a fog. I hadn't finished! That feeling never left me and I died with it. I was furious!

Pause.

I was a good Party supporter. My man had talked to me about death. We had agreed on a system that we could understand whereby the atoms of the body are liberated by death and stream off to rejoin the other atoms in the infinite universe. They then get back into organic matter – we never quite worked out how – and take part in the eternal play of the universe's life, probably unconscious of ourselves, just fizzing about somehow. Let me tell you, that is all so much rubbish. I still don't know it all, but I know that I am what I was. To describe where I am is impossible because you do not have any experience of the dimensions – it is outside, but inside. You, in that room, have turned out the light to see me. You have made yourselves blind. So might you well have done, for you are. The natural world is the body beneath the skin you squat on now. Imagination can reach me, which is how we've met again. This fraud, this glass sliding over the table I ate off so often, is enough of an effort. For you it was an enormous task to get this far, to take the risk of me appearing…and now you're not so sure, are you? Science is more comfortable. Sonia makes you turn away. The joy of reunion lasts a couple of minutes, and then the soreness comes back, the eyes don't quite meet, the chair is slightly angled away.

Pause.

You laughed at me often enough. Forty, flirting, hanging round the famous lads with the new ideas, trying to get in on everything and what did I get? Sonia, we need uniforms for the Novgorod branch. We should have uniforms. Here's a design for you. Do you understand the drawing? Here's our budget. It's not much but we know you can manage. With training like your mother gave you, you could put uniforms on the backs of the whole Bolshevik army and still have remnants for a few flags.

Pause.

Having a first child at that age was dangerous, Mamushka. I didn't need to ask around. I remembered the Jewess, thirty-seven wasn't she? Dead. And others. Yet I was putting it off for later.

Laughs.

Where did I get that idea from? That there was always a later. That my body would respond to that *later*. I believed it, oh yes, and I believed it because I was rubbing shoulders with miracles every day, and putting flashes on their lapels and red stars on their cuffs. *Later* was the eternal future and we were already living in it. There was no present, no past – only this future which we were balanced on the edge of, like a child on a passing cart steals a ride. So, where are we now? Sixteen years later, Mamushka, and you have two sons missing, another in prison, all the sea of your family is pouring out of the hole in the wall which I made. You are in that future of mine, and you know it. So you ask me what is going on?

Pause.

The ikon again. It is still there. They have allowed the
ikons to remain because they are useful in prodding the
memory towards one truth which is the same at any
time, anywhere. Sacrifice works. You give, the black air
accepts and passes your few bits of gold dust onto the
banker whose vault is churningly empty, groaning,
always asking for more. Mamushka, it is not my future
you have here. What has happened is that the present has
reasserted itself, and teamed up with the past. The future
is in the tin box in the Neva. My brothers have been
taken by the police because they come from a house with
closed curtains and empty glasses which sing an
unscientific song. Turn on the light, open the door to the
street and see clearly in the new darkness. The future is
over, but it will come again. No! I said no questions!
Stalin will die when Stalin will die. Ten years, twenty
years, a thousand years. Such a lack of interest now.
That's what I miss about you. You're so practical. Let us
summon Sonia she'll never come and ask her about the
boys.

Pause.

You've seen me, haven't you Mamushka? In the kitchen?
Laying the table? Climbing the stairs to bed – not that
you ever saw me doing that for I was always the last up.
Asking for me wasn't difficult, was it? You did it all my
life. This house smells of me still. The rugs are where I
laid them, the cups where I hung them, the log-pile
where I laid it. Leave the glass aside. It hasn't been
washed properly. What a family you are! Helpless! Even
now you cannot take care of yourselves. No one has
taken up where I left off. You depend upon the past as if
the meals come from the museum. I never left the house!
Our three boys are in trouble because they could not
keep up with change. If asked for a line on something
they always answered – give us the policies. And when
there are no policies, when someone is dreaming them
up at that very moment, you've got to have a better
answer. I used to say – keep your fingers crossed,

something will turn up, or even, the Party will provide, for a joke. That way you'll get away with not knowing, but your sons think like slaves. That's why they get treated like slaves. They couldn't keep up with the alterations. Ask anyone who's done any sewing on a large scale what the biggest bugbear is – it's keeping up with the alterations. This isn't the kind of stuff you wanted from your Sonia, is it? You really can't stand talking politics. Well, you should be happy enough now – nineteen thirty-seven in Novgorod, you don't talk politics, everyone smiles. That's your new language, the smile.

Angrily.

Why did you let those boys grow up such thickheads? You can teach survival. There is imagination in all of them if you'd only left a hole for it to get out. They could have given dancing answers. But what did they do, great blockheads? Of course I know what's right. One two three. Sorry comrade. One and three are correct, but two is treacherously wrong. My answer would have been, I wait each day for advice on how I should progress towards…the future. So, Svetlana is leaving. Goodbye Svetlana. I saw you fidgeting and throwing out hints that I'd overstayed my welcome. Well, at least the woman can still take action, even if it's walking out on this kind of experience. I brought her up right, even if I say so myself. Best thing she can do is tell herself this never happened – one of those deep winter vodka nightmares when the ice gets on top of you.

Pause.

Did you ever miss me? Did the Party ever miss me? Did my child ever miss me? In a big family like ours, you don't get missed, you get healed over. From now on you will be worried about spying, that I will know all the secret things you do, and think. You will have no privacy. When you believed in God, Mamushka, you also believed that he wasn't nosey; I think you would extend that to your eldest daughter who is now in a position of power. But I'm not. You can see more of me than I can of you. You, though it's difficult to credit, have more life than I have. You can change things. I could not even find you a linen tablecloth, and I know how scarce they are. You are still frightened of me, and I don't blame you, for you can see how the woman in me is diminished. I do no needlework now. My arms go round no great shoulders, I do not discuss death with lovers.

Pause.

Help will come for you. There will be war to break things open again. The young men will want war. That will change things. We know war will come. A favour, Mamushka. A favour before I go. Yes, I must, or you will all be caught and punished. Will you dance for me? You don't need music. We never did. Here, in Russia, music is everywhere. It comes out of the ground, out of the trees, out of our skins. Music. If I am anything at all out there it is a rough old song. Sonia. You can sing me again and again when Sonia needs remembering. Can you hear me? That note in the air? The stove hisses. The ice cries out around the window. The marching men coming down the road are whistling at me. We heard Sonia was here. Come on, dance! No, not those old, sad steps. New ones! Make them up as you go along. Improvise, for God's sake! Stir yourselves! Think! Imagine a fresh dance. No, no, don't dance on the floor. Get up on the table! Mark it for me with the nails in your shoes. Yes, scratch it so that every time you eat I stare you in the face and say later is too late. Live now! Dance! Dance! Dance! Dmitri is dancing down the pathway. The soldiers are dancing through the gate. Stalin is dancing to his grave. Russia is dancing for Sonia, and moving again!

Lights fade fast. Blackout.

The End.